SEASONS
SOUTH AND NORTH

TEACHING GLOBAL NATURE

Anne Morddel

INTRODUCTION

It is a basic element of early education for children to learn about seasons and how the natural world around them changes through the year's cycle. Yet almost no books exist at the early years level about the seasons of the Southern Hemisphere or about comparing the seasons and nature of the Southern with the Northern Hemispheres.

I wrote and illustrated *The Big Field : A Child's Year Under the Southern Cross* to tell young children of the wonderful world of vines, flowers, trees, birds, insects, and butterflies in the Southern Hemisphere, specifically in the Atlantic Rainforest of Brazil.

This book of activities and lesson plans does not need to accompany *The Big Field : A Child's Year Under the Southern Cross* but it will be enhanced by it. I hope that you and your children will find in this book activities to enjoy that will inspire you to discover more of our planet's beautiful natural world.

Anne Morddel

a.morddel@yahoo.com

CONTENTS

The Big Field and Primary Curriculum Subjects

The Big Field ties in with the following Primary Curriculum Subjects:

<u>Geography</u>

<u>Solar system</u>

Earth's orbit and rotation cause changes in weather and the seasons in the Southern and Northern Hemispheres

<u>Weather</u>

Fog

Winds

Storms

Weather around the world : Southern Brazil, Atlantic Rainforest weather

<u>Land use</u>

Agricultural history, burning a forest to make a farm, different crops

<u>Places</u>

Brazil, Paranã, Mata Atlantica (additionally, Argentina, Uruguay, Paraguay)

Science: <u>Life processes and living things</u>

                            Birds

                            Minibeasts

                            Birds that eat minibeasts

                            Green Plants :

                                    gathering seeds

                                    planting seeds

                                    birds that plant seeds

                                    trees, especially flowering trees

                                    seeds that we use

                                    fruit

                            Animal homes

                            Migration

<u>General History :</u>   <u>Ourselves and our families</u>

                            Grandparents and their parents and grandparents,
                                    brothers and sisters

                            Emigration to South America from Europe and
                                    the changes in the environment caused by
                                    the incoming farmers

<u>Art:</u>   <u>Making things</u>

SUBJECTS GENERAL TO THE STORY AS A WHOLE

Geography – The story of *The Big Field* takes place in the state of Paraná, in Southern Brazil. (25S 14 40, 49W 26 18 are the latitude and longitude for the capitol of the state, Curitiba). A number of plants and birds are also found in the neighbouring South American countries of Argentina, Paraguay and Uruguay.

Seasons – *The Big Field* is a book of the months of the year, linked to the seasons as they occur in the Southern Hemisphere. During discussions about the orbit of the earth around the sun and of the Earth's tilt on its axis, it can be explained to children that the seasons occur in the same order in the Northern and Southern Hemispheres, but during different months of the year. While, nearer the equator, there is little noticeable difference between seasons, further south, the differences are quite marked.

Summer months: December, January, February

Autumn months: March, April, May

Winter months: June, July, August

Spring months: September, October, November

It is worth noting that children in Brazil begin the school year at the end of Summer, usually in late February or early March. Thus, during their Summer holidays, they also have Christmas, Hanukah, and the New Year.

Atlantic Rainforest – "The Atlantic Forest (*Mata Atlântica* in Portuguese) is a region of tropical and subtropical moist forest, tropical dry forest, tropical savannas, and mangrove forests which extends along the Atlantic coast of Brazil from Rio Grande do Norte state in the north to Rio Grande do Sul state in the south, and inland as far as Paraguay and the Misiones Province of Argentina.

"The Atlantic Forest is now designated a World Biosphere Reserve, which contains a large number of highly endangered species. It has been extensively cleared since colonial times. The remnant is estimated to be less than 10% of the original and that is often broken into hilltop islands." (Adapted from the article on Wikipedia)

The Big Field takes place on a farm at the edge of the Atlantic Rainforest. All of the animals, trees and flowers in the story aretaken from sightings in or very near to the Atlantic Rainforest. All are placed in the month during which they were sighted. Nearly all of the species present in the story have been identified, in English and with the Latin names, enabling teachers to find more information on them for use in class work.

A key aspect of the story is the grandmother's dedication to replanting the rainforest on the Big Field. It is her knowledge and love of the nature that she passes on to her grandchild through play and through replanting.

Useful websites for background on the Atlantic Rainforest :

www.sosmatatlantica.org.br - Portuguese only, this is a major
environmental protection organization.

www.spvs.org.br - With an English page, this a the site of an
organization dedicated to conservation of the Atlantic
Rainforest

www.iracambi.com - an excellent historical perspective on how
European farming led to the destruction of the
rainforest, with projects for reversing the trend and
opportunities for involvement.

https://www.nature.org/en-us/get-involved/how-to-help/places-we-protect/atlantic-forest/
The Nature Conservancy has a very good section on the
Atlantic Rainforest and its work there.

www.institutoterra.org In English and Portuguese, this organization is
doing exactly the same as the Granny in *The Big Field* :
replanting the native species of the Atlantic Rainforest
on land from which it had been stripped away.

Science and the Environment – There is a very wide scope for learning more about birds, butterflies, insects, trees and plants with *The Big Field*. Each illustration contains at least one bird, butterfly and insect.

Internet research:

Of the innumerable possibilities, I found those listed below to be most pertinent and helpful, as well as attractive and entertaining.

At the time of going to press, Wikipedia had an article on every species listed in *The Big Field*.

N.B. When searching on the Internet for any of the species, the best results are obtained if the Latin name is used, in quotes.

www.theseedsite.co.uk - An excellent site, all about seeds, with pictures of many. It also has a section for teachers with links to topics of the National Curriculum Key Stages in Science, and a Junior Seed Site.

www.zsl.org/london-zoo - As always, superb, with many of the bird, butterfly and insect species mentioned in the story.

https://www.hbw.com/ibc - This is The Internet Bird Collection, a wonderful website which has many of the bird species, with photographs and very nice videos of them.

www.bugguide.net - Good pictures of insects, very little discussion.

www.arthurgrosset.com - An excellent site on birds of the region.

YEAR-LONG ACTIVITIES

Start an Atlantic Rainforest Garden – Many seed companies sell the species listed in the story, with recommendations as to where and how to plant them. If a greenhouse is available, or if your school is in a tropical climate, everything mentioned in the story can be planted. In the event that an uncovered plot in a cold region is all that is available, there are still quite a number of plants listed that would grow in colder climates.

Species Shelf – Collect on outings or from the school garden pieces of bark, seeds, leaves, flowers, etc. Make small signs with both the English and Latin names.

North-South Seasons Table – On a low table or shelf, create a scene made from flowers, leaves, seeds, indicative of your local season. Have the children draw and make paper models of the trees, flowers, birds, insects, etc. that appear in the season at that time in *The Big Field*.

Visits to Botanical Gardens, Insect Houses, Aviaries – If at all possible, try to take the children to where they will see the plants and animals of *The Big Field*. A tropical garden greenhouse in a Botanical Garden,   especially, will give them the feel of the warm, humid atmosphere. The London Zoo has many, many of the insects, butterflies and birds from this story. They can be found in the Blackburn Pavilion, B.U.G.S., the Butterfly Paradise, and others.

Observation Charts – To encourage observational skills, create a chart for each animal of interest (birds, butterflies, insects) with an example from eachhemisphere for each month. The children can draw or find pictures of what they have seen in their own environment. This can be done as a large poster or as individual charts. They should be on display during the year.

MONTH-BY-MONTH
SUBJECTS, PLANT AND ANIMAL SPECIES, AND ACTIVITIES

THE STORY'S BEGINNING PAGE

<u>Subjects</u> :

Parents who both work full time – this is not discussed but mentioned and could be the foundation of a brief classroom discussion wherein the children talk of their own parents' jobs. Here, the grandmother is the carer for the children.

Family relationships – Siblings, parents, grandparent, great- grandparent - There are three children in the story. The narrator, who remains nameless and unidentified, is the eldest. Chloe is next, Baby is the last. The grandmother mentions her own father and grandfather, providing an opportunity of discussions of family lineage and relationships of three and four generations.

Land use – The grandmother tells of how her grandfather burned the original forest to create a field where he planted coffee and soybeans. Her father burned again and planted again. This follows the pattern of destruction of most of the forests of the world today, including those of the Amazon region and Indonesia. The planting of coffee and then soybeans follows the historical pattern of land use near Curitiba, the capitol of the state of Paranã in Brazil. Coffee grown there could not compete with that grown in other parts of the country and was replaced with soybeans. Paranã is now one of the largest soybean producing regions of the world.

<u>Animal Species:</u>

Bird: Great Kiskadee (Pitangus sulphuratus)

The Great Kiskadee is common everywhere in Brazil. There, its name is "bem-ti-vi", which means "Good to see you" in Portuguese. It has a loud, three-note cry that lilts on the third note. It is as familiar to Brazilian children as are sparrows to North American children.

Butterfly: White peacock (Anartia jatrophe)

It could be of interest to the children to compare photographs of this butterfly with the American peacock butterfly (Papilio orythia).

Caterpillar:

Unidentified. Seen in the forest near the Iguaçú Falls.

<u>Plant Species</u>

Border vine: Coastal Morning Glory (Ipomea cairica)

This is a type of morning glory, with very large mauve or white
flowers. It twines and heaps along roadsides. Here, it is a bit
golden, as it appears on a sunny late afternoon.

Small pink flowers:
Unidentified. Seen growing among grasses on a sandy beach in
the Summer.

<u>Suggested Activities</u>

Visit – To a farm with chickens, to the insect section of a zoo, or to their websites

Map making – make a map showing where the Atlantic Rainforest once was and one
showing what remains now. Alternatively, make a map of Brazil, locating the state of
Paranã.

JANUARY

<u>Subjects:</u>

Astronomy – Not truly a primary school subject, this could come under Geography. As the North Star is so familiar to children in the Northern Hemisphere, the Southern Cross is just as familiar to children in the Southern Hemisphere. Here, the name of the grandmother's farm is "Southern Cross".

<u>Animal Species</u>

Bird: Blue Dacnis   (Dacnis)

This little bird has a "bandit mask", very similar to the nuthatch.

Butterfly: Mourning rose   (Papilio anchisiades)

Small butterflies: Mandana metalmark   (Emesis mandana)

Spider:

Unidentified. Seen in the forest near the Iguaçú Falls.

<u>Plant Species</u>

Border: Cestrum   (Cestrum corymbosum)

As with many of the plants in the border illustrations, and as with many lovely wildflowers, this is considered a weed. If the children are of an age to understand, it would be worth discussing what makes a plant or insect "valuable" to people, and to point out that farmers, tourists, and artists have differing wishes and therefore differing views.

<u>Activities:</u>

Stargazing – Where night activities are permitted and a telescope available, try to locate the North Star or the Southern Cross.

Observation Calendar – Begin a monthly calendar where children bring in or draw insects that they have seen in their gardens or parks that month. The same could be done with butterflies or birds.

Make a bandit mask – like those that seem to be on the Blue Dacnis.

FEBRUARY

<u>Subjects:</u>

Science - Rainforests – The kapok tree is mentioned as one of the tallest of trees. Explanation of the three canopies of rainforests would include the kapok.

<u>Animal Species</u>

Bird:	Tropical kingbird	(Tyrannus melancholicus)
Butterfly:	Blue night butterfly	(Cepheuptychia cephus)
Insect:	Leaf cutter ants	(Atta sexsdens)

Many farmers greatly dislike these ants, for they can destroy crops rapidly. In the story, the Granny is a bit unusual in seeing their role as something good. She sees them as useful in the same way that dung beetles are, in that they clean up something. www.wildernessclassroom.com has a page with a good description and pictures of leaf cutter ants.

<u>Plant Species</u>

Border: Morning Glory   (Ipomea nil)

Tree: Ear tree or umbrella tree (Enterolobium
                         contortisiliquum)

Depicted in the illustration as an umbrella, the umbrella tree
does make a large, umbrella-shaped canopy.

Flowers: Kapok tree (Chorisia speciosa)

The kapok tree's large, pink, white and yellow, star-shaped
flowers cascade from the trees in late Summer and cover the
ground at the base of the trees. Here, they are being cut and
taken away in morsels by leaf-cutter ants.

<u>Activities:</u>

Make a study of tree trunks and their bark – They are all different and usually full of
interesting insects. Collect some pieces from the ground and take them back for your
species shelf.

Make trugs – From paper or card. Fill them with seeds and plant the seeds.

MARCH

<u>Subjects</u>

Family relationships – Siblings – The Baby cries quite a lot. The children in the class could discuss their own younger brothers and sisters who may also cry often.

Science – Male cicadas make the loud, "EEEEEEEEEE!!!!!" noise that can be quite deafening where they are numerous. They make the noise by vibrating membrane-like structures on their abdomens (males have larger abdomens than females). The cicada species in the story is much larger than most, averaging seven centimeters in length. www.cicadamania.com has a wealth of rather unusual cicada information.

Science – Flowering trees - At this time many trees in the Northern Hemisphere are beginning to flower and a comparison between the colours and sizes of the flowers of trees of the two Hemispheres could be made.

Geography – Weather - Seasons - The Autumnal Equinox is in March. Gradually, the weather will grow cooler.

<u>Animal Species</u>

    Bird: Green-headed tanager   (Tangara seledon)

These beautiful small birds are easily tamed, as they will do just about anything for a banana. www.arthurgrosset.com has some very nice pictures.

    Butterfly: Common Morpho   (Morpho helenor violaceus)

The blue Morpho butterfly is one of the best-known creatures of Brazil. It is iridescent, and easily the size of the breadth of a child's hand. In the forest, their flight seems more like wafting or floating. A pay-to-use site, www.enchantedlearning.com has a picture of a Morpho that can be printed out and coloured.

Insect: Cicada   (Fidicina mannifera)

See above, in *Science* for this month.

Plant Species

Border: Red Tasselflower   (Emilia sonchifolia)

A tiny, bright flower, considered a weed and a medicine. www.botanypictures.com has good pictures of it.

Flower: Lenten Tree   (Tibouchina granulosa rosea)

In cultivation, the Lenten Tree's flowers can be deep purple, but in the Atlantic Rainforest, they are of the pink variety, and they stand out against the green of the surrounding forest. The name in both English and Portuguese ("Quaresmeira") comes from the fact that it blooms during the time of the Christian observation of Lent.

Flowers for the mobile: St. John's Bread Tree   (Inga sessilis)

Fruit: Common banana

Activities

Make a mobile from flowers – either real flowers or paper. To copy the ingã flowers, tie together fifteen strips of light yellow ribbon, with a knot at the top.

Cicada Shriek – Have all of the children shriek "EEEEE!!!" as high and as long as their breath will hold. It still will not be as high or as loud or as long as the real thing.

APRIL

<u>Subjects</u>

Geography – Land Use - The oranges are ripe and ready for harvest during this month. It is an opportunity to discuss harvesting on farms. Additionally, two invasive species are shown in this month, the Rhinoceros beetle and the spadeleaf. Invasive species do so well in their new environment that they crowd out or kill off native species.

Trees and their seeds – The seeds of many trees begin to fall in April. It is when the Granny can collect many, many seeds to replant her forest, and is roughly equal to when acorns begin to fall in the Northern Hemisphere. The long, bumpy seedpod of the golden medallion tree will grow to a tall tree with golden balls of flowers. This tree is shown in the picture for the month of November.

<u>Animal Species</u>

Bird: Trogon   (Trogon surrucua)

This bird is not very shy. It has large eyes with a ring around them, making them seem even larger. It will perch quite close to a human and stare most disconcertingly.

Butterfly: Lacewing   (Actinote sp.)

Insect: Rhinoceros beetle   (Oryctes nasicornis)

This is one of the few non-native, invasive species in the book. It is native to Europe, but can be found throughout Southern Brazil. www.treknature.com has a big picture and a good description of it, mentioning that it is the strongest animal in the world, in terms of weight-carrying ability.

<u>Plant Species</u>

Border: Spadeleaf   (Centella asiatica)

This species is another invasive species that is originally from Asia but is now found everywhere in Brazil.

Flower: Yesterday-Today-and-Tomorrow

(Brunfelsis pauciflora)

The way that this plant flowers is fascinating. The flowers open as dark, then fade, until they are white. All the shades from dark to light can be present on the bush at the same time. It is   native to the Atlantic Rainforest and grows easily in other places. Pretty as it is, this plant would be a good choice for the Atlantic Rainforest garden ONLY if it is in a protected area as the berries are poisonous to humans.

Large Seed: Golden medallion tree   (Cassia leptophyla)

The seedpods are from 25 to 35 centimeters long, and each seed is the size of a ping-pong ball.

Fruit: Ordinary Orange

Brazil is one of the largest orange-producing countries in the world.

<u>Activities</u>

Make a Golden medallion tree seedpod – Have each child crumple thick paper into balls and fold them into a pod of heavy brown paper and glue it shut.

Insect pets – by now, it is clear that Chloe loves insects. Have each child draw or model from clay an insect they would like to have as a pet. Display them all on the Species Shelf.

MAY

<u>Subjects</u>

Science – Trees for food, trees for warmth - The massive kapok tree, also called "silk floss tree", (Chorisia speciosa) produces egg-shaped seedpods about 15 centimeters long that crack open when they fall to the ground, releasing a soft, luxuriantly silky fluff. This fluff contains the actual seeds and is a major food for the parakeets that are as common as sparrows, even in the cities. The first Europeans quickly learned to use it as the filling for quilts, quilted clothing, mattresses, pillows, and cushions. Many older people in the countryside carry on the tradition. The flowers of this tree are shown in the illustration for the month of February. www.floridata.com has a good picture of the tree, its flowers, and its VERY spiny trunk.

Science – Decreased habitats for wild creatures – As humans encroach upon and destroy more and more of nature, that last hidden species are being forced out of hiding. Numerous recent news stories of newly discovered animals attest to this. The invasion of moths, which had never been seen before, is another example of this. In truth, they appeared because a large part of virgin forest nearby has been bulldozed to build a shopping mall. As *The Big Field* is positive and about hope and what can be done to help bring back habitats, there is no discussion, other than at the very beginning, of the destruction that makes this so urgently necessary.

<u>Animal Species</u>

    Bird: Plain Parakeet   (Brotogeris tirica)

As mentioned above, these parakeets are numerous, and fly in large, noisy flocks, even in the cities. They are very keen on the kapok seeds.

    Butterfly: Helicon   (Heliconius ethilla narcaea)

    Insect: Moth   (Hemiceras)

See above, *Science – Decreased habitats for wild creatures*

<u>Plant Species</u>

Border: Falling Autumn leaves

These are of no specific species, just brown leaves falling in Autumn.

Seedpod: Kapok or Silk Floss Tree   (Chorisia speciosa)

See above : *Science – Trees for food, trees for warmth*

<u>Activities</u>

Raking leaves and rolling in the leaf pile – This is an Autumn activity of children everywhere in the world. Are there leaves to rake in May where you are? Can you make some from paper? Children in the Northern Hemisphere probably roll in leaves without fear, but children in Paranã can do so only in the Autumn. In the Spring and Summer a VERY DANGEROUS caterpillar lurks in fallen leaves. (See the month of December.)

Start quilting or cushion making – Some companies, such as <u>www.greenfibres.com</u>, sell untreated kapok. If you can purchase a bag of that, and some ordinary quilting batting, the children can see and feel the difference. Have each child bring from home some fabric to work the cushion or class quilt.

Observation of birds and trees – What birds can the children observe in your area eating from the trees or shrubs nearby? Encourage them to look. If there is nature out of the classroom window, spend some time as a class gazing out of the window, perhaps with binoculars. Try to identify the birds and the names of the plants that are their food.

JUNE

<u>Subjects</u>

Science -Birds that plant trees/Seed dispersal – The story told by Granny is told everywhere in the region and is true. Just as the Bluejay of North America will bury acorns, so the Azure jay will bury the seeds of the Paranã pine. They both forget some, and many of those grow to trees.

Science – Different kinds of pine trees – The Paranã pine is also called the "parasol pine" but is not to be confused with the much small Mediterranean tree of the same name. www.conifers.org not only has very good pictures of this tree, its seed ball, and the Azure jay, but a lovely reminiscence by an elderly Brazilian (in English) of growing up among such pines and eating the seeds.

History – Midsummer bonfires in mid-Winter – a colonial transplant – June 24th Is St. John's Day in the Christian religion. It also is Midsummer's Day in the Northern Hemisphere, anciently celebrated with great bonfires at night. The European immigrants carried that tradition to Brazil, where St. John's Day bonfires are now on cold Winter nights, blending religion, midwinter, and harvest celebrations into one big festival called Festa Junina.

Geography – Country and state symbols from nature. – Here, two state symbols, the Azure jay and the Paranã pine, are introduced. More appear later. Nearly all such symbols are from nature, not man-made creations.

Animal Species

Bird: Azure Jay (Cyanocorax caeruleus)

This bird is so much a part of the Atlantic Rainforest that it was named the state bird of Paranã.

Butterfly: Orsis bluewing (Myscelia orsis)

Many butterflies survive in the cities, but this one cannot and is found only in forested and wooded areas.

Insect: Angular wing katydid (Microcentrum)

Another of Chloe's insect pets.

Plant Species

Border: Viscum (Loranthacea)

This is a parasite that lives on many trees, twining around their trunks and branches. Each tiny leaf has a very intricate pattern of black lines on it.

Tree and Seed: Paranã pine (Araucaria angustifolia)

This pine can grow to 40 meters and is an integral part of the Atlantic Rainforest. It is the state tree of Paranã.

<u>Activities</u>

Drawing Pine trees – Children of Paranã, if asked to draw a tree, will sketch something that to a foreigner looks like a stick with a plate balanced on top – a Paranã pine. Have your class try to draw the pine tree familiar to them and then a Paranã pine.

Compare pine nuts – It may not be easy to obtain seed of the Paranã pine (though some seed catalogues have them) but it is very easy to buy a package of pine nuts in any Italian foods store. Compare these tiny Northern Hemisphere seeds with the much larger ones from the Southern Hemisphere. WARNING : SOME CHILDREN ARE ALLERGIC TO NUTS. IT IS RECOMMENDED TO KEEP THEM IN A PACKAGE.

Symbols – The Azure Jay and the Paranã pine are state symbols of the state of Paranã, because they were once so prolific there that they were identified with the place. What is your state's symbol? How does it compare with those of Paranã? Have the children try to find them in their surroundings.

JULY

<u>Subjects</u>

Geography - Houses and homes – The grandmother mentions three types of animal home: a nest, a den, an earth, and compares them to a house. She says that all are "more than shelter", they are a home. She describes what in Spanish is called "querencia" , the deep instinct that will take an animal to its home, the place it feels safe.

Geography – Weather – Fog – All of the Atlantic Rainforest can be very foggy at times. In the Winter, the fog can be very thick and cold. It does not rain much in the Winter; there is just a succession of days of deep, freezing fog, when the trees drip moisture. In Paranã, the Atlantic Rainforest is a temperate rainforest. It receives a large amount of rain and its fog comes from it being close to the coast. The fog is so dense that it can bring another 30 centimeters per year of precipitation.

Geography – Seasons – Winter – Winter is the dry season, in that it does not rain during July and August. It can be very cold, even reach freezing, though not for long.

Geography – Country and state symbols from nature – The Rufus hornero is the national bird for Argentina.

Science – Animal homes – Bird nests – The ovenbird builds its nest of mud on branches. If its habitat is very crowded, it will even build on top of another ovenbird's mud nest.

<u>Animal Species</u>

Bird: Rufus hornero or Ovenbird (Furnarius rufus)

This bird has rather dull colouring. It is interesting for its unusual nest building. It is unmistakable for its loud, raucous call. www.arthurgrosset.com has a good information page with pictures of the bird and its nest. It is the national bird of Argentina.

Butterfly: Brazilian Skipper   (Calpodes ethlius)

Insect:

          Unidentified fly with transparent wings, seen in Curitiba.

<u>Plant Species</u>

Border: Morning Glory   (ipomea carnea, subs. Fistulosa)

Blue flower: Morning Glory   (Ipomea purpurea)

Plants on the branches: Bromeliads   (Bromelia)

<u>Activities</u>

Build an ovenbird's nest - With clay, have the children shape a nest like the ovenbird's.

Symbols – The Rufus hornero is the national bird of Argentina. If it was not possible to do the symbols activity of the previous month, it is repeated here. What is your state's symbol? How does it compare to those of Paranã and Argentina? Have the children try to find your bird or tree in their surroundings.

Learn about morning glories – By now, four different varieties of morning glory have appeared in *The Big Field*: Ipomea cairica at the beginning of the story, ipomea nil in February, and ipomea carnea and purpurea, both in July. Plant a few seeds of ipomea or find some in a garden nearby. Show the children how it binds other plants and chokes them but also how very pretty the flowers can be. When plants are unwanted, they are called weeds and people go to extreme measures to kill them. When the same plant is wanted, it is called a flower, and people will go to great measures to cultivate and protect them. There are no good or bad plants (not even those that are poisonous) there are only peoples' desires to have them or be rid of them.

Explain fog – Show the children how fog is a product of cold air over hot air with the demonstration on www.weatherwizkids.com

AUGUST

<u>Subjects</u>

Science – Birds – Lapwings – Lapwings do not occur in North America, but they are related to plovers. Southern Lapwings are waders, though they spend much time on grass, even around airport runways, they nest on the ground, and will swoop and dive acrobatically at those who come too close to their nests and can be quite aggressive about it.

Geography - Winds – In South America, the cold winds come from the south, with August having many days of bitterly cold wind.

<u>Animal Species</u>

Bird: Southern lapwing (Vanellus chilensis)

The national bird of Uruguay. www.arthurgrosset.com has many good pictures of this bird.

Butterfly :   Swallowtail   (Papilio sp.)

Compare this swallowtail with the much-loved North American species.

Upper insect: Walking stick or Stick insect (Phasmatodea)

These are rarely seen in gardens or cities, but it is not necessary to go very deep into the woods to find them.

Lower insect: Millipede   (Diplopoda)

It is not necessary at all to look far for these insects, as they often enter houses and get trapped on carpets, where they are found in the morning, waiting to be rescued.

<u>Plant Species</u>

Border: Wissadula   (Wissadula subpeltata)

This is another plant that has been labeled as a weed.

<u>Activities</u>

Make kites – Children all over the world enjoy flying kites, and they are very easy to make: two sticks, some glue, paper, and string.

Finish the quilting projects – make a presentation – see the activities for the month of May, above.

SEPTEMBER

<u>Subjects</u>

Science – Birds – Migration – Many birds migrate seasonally between South and North America, such as the swallow (see October, below). www.backyardnature.net has a good page explaining bird migration between the Americas, albeit from the North American point of view. This subject continues into October, when the swallows return from the North.

Geography – Seasons – Signs of Spring – Now is one of the times when the difference between the seasons in the Northern Hemisphere and the Southern Hemisphere is most obvious. In the North, Summer is ending and seeds are falling. In the South, migratory birds are returning and flowers are beginning to bloom. September is the month of the Vernal Equinox in the Southern Hemisphere.

<u>Animal Species</u>

Bird: Rufus-bellied thrush (Turdus rufiventris)

The national bird of Brazil, and much loved by all Brazilians. Its song is lovely and for this reason, though it is rather dull to look at, many Brazilians keep a thrush in a cage at home. It can live as long as 25 to 30 years. Stories, poems and songs have been written about the *larangeira* (pronounced la-ran-JAIR-uh). The bird flies north as far as the Amazon region during the Winter, and its return to the south in September is a much-loved sign of Spring.

Bird with long tail: Fork-tailed flycatcher (Tyrannus savanna)

This is also called the scissor-tailed flycatcher or, in Portuguese, the scissor bird. It Winters in the Amazon Basin and returns south in the Spring. It is a common sight, in the   early evening all Summer, to see these birds swooping and diving over puddles or lakes or swimming pools, catching mosquitoes and flies.

On www.whatbird.com , you can hear a recording of the bird's call.

Butterfly: Flame   (Dryas Julia)

A magically bright and beautiful butterfly. The Wikipedia article has a picture of the caterpillar as well.

Snail: Tree snail   (Drymaeus sp.)

These get to be quite big, up to seven centimeters long, as big as a baby's foot.

Plant Species

Border: Dayflower   (Commelina erecta)

This little plant grows easily and everywhere. Its leaves are often put in salads.

Tree: Yellow Ipê   (Tabebuia chrysotricha)

Also called the Golden Trumpet tree, this is the national tree of Brazil. Its bright yellow blossoms cover the tree in the Spring and it truly is folkloric that "when the ipê blooms, Winter is over". The sight of a tree in full bloom is breathtaking. Sadly, this tree is now at risk because garden furniture is being made from it and sold around the world. Please do not buy Ipê furniture!

<u>Activities</u>

Learn bird calls – Find recordings of some of the birds and let the children have a fun time shrieking in imitation.

Make maps of migration routes - Let each child make a simple map of migration routes between the Americas.

Roll down a grassy hill - Is this permitted anymore? Alternatively, get your hands on a couple of meters of artificial grass and let the children roll across that. In truth, it will feel about as scratchy as the grass in Brazil, some species of which are so sharp as to cut one's feet and which are planted around houses to deter barefoot thieves.

Make fog – Repeat the fog explanation activity from July, above. Then, let a humidifier fill a small room with fog. Go in with the children until it is suffocating and see how wonderful it feels to come out. That is how it feels when the fog finally stops, the ipê blooms, the birds return and Winter is truly over.

Signs of seasons art – Remind the children of the signs of Spring in their environment and compare them with those listed in September. Have them draw their favourite signs of Spring.

OCTOBER

<u>Subjects</u>

Science – Birds and Insects – Food - The Winged termite is everywhere in the Atlantic Rainforest and in the farmlands that now cover the land where the forest once was. They build tall earth mounds for nests. A mound can be one to one and a half meters high, as tall as a six-year-old child. (Thus, they are often considered a nuisance and their nests are knocked down with sticks or run down with tractors. Useless, for they can rebuild the mound in a night.) When the heavy rains come in mid-Spring, the mounds are flooded and the termites swarm into the sky. At just this time, the swallows return to the South from the North, and engage in a feeding frenzy at the termite swarm. To those who live there, it is one of the most common and indicative natural occurrences in the month of October.

<u>Animal Species</u>

Bird: Bare-throated bell-bird (Procnias nudicollis)

The national bird of Paraguay. When this bird's call is heard for the first time, ringing out in the forest, one cannot believe it is a bird. At the time of going to press, there was a short film of a bell-bird making its call on YouTube. www.arthurgrosset.com has photographs and a description.

Butterfly:

Unidentified. Seen in the forest at Iguaçú Falls.

Small flying birds: Blue-and-white swallow
(Notiochelidon cyanoleuca)

Insect:

Unidentified. Seen in the forest along the Estrada da Graciosa near Morretes.

Tiny flying insect: Winged termite   (Isoptera)

<u>Plant Species</u>

Border: Creeping Fig   (Ficus pumila)

This little vine is planted to cover every garden wall and many buildings. Every Brazilian child is familiar with it.

Tree: Tiger's claw tree   (Erythrina falcata)

The national tree of both Argentina and Uruguay. "Tiger's claw tree" is its name in English, and the children can see why. As there are no tigers in Brazil, to which to compare its flowers, its name in Portuguese means "Parrot's beak tree". It flowers in late Winter and Spring. The rains of October dash all of its blossoms to the ground. The flowers are sturdy and a bit rubbery, so children play with them.

<u>Activities</u>

Make the bell-bird's cry – Take any gong-like instruments, or even heavy cooking pots, and let the children beat on them with wooden spoons. The bell-bird opens its mouth incredibly wide in order to make its gong sound. Show the children the YouTube clip of the bird, and have them listen to some of the recordings of it on www.xeno-canto.org , then let them throw back their heads and do their best to make the same sound.

Build a termite hill – The children could either build individual termite hills out of plain, brown clay or the class could build a large hill out of papier maché. If the latter, they could with pipe cleaners also make numerous Winged termites.

NOVEMBER

<u>Subjects</u>

Science – Dangerous insects – There are two extremely dangerous insects in the Southern part of the Atlantic Rainforest: the brown spider and the Lonomia caterpillar. The spider's bite can leave open sores that do not heal, requiring hospitalization and possibly surgery. The Lonomia caterpillar, shown in December, can kill. Every child is taught from a very early age to identify these two insects, to know when and where to look for them, and to avoid places where they might be found. Efforts to eradicate them with poisons have not been too successful. Most homes with gardens, even in the cities, keep a few chickens, as they are the best predator of both the spider and the caterpillar.

Science – Ecology – Encouraging local plants – The Tillandsia stricta, sometimes called the "air plant" is native to the region. They grow on just about anything that will support them. They are epiphytes and thus do not require soil to grow. They get their nutrients from air and water through their leaves. Like lichens in the North, they cannot grow where the air is too polluted. In *The Big Field* the Granny and children make little platforms to hang for the tillandsia stricta to grow. With many species, all that is needed is to provide a place for them to live, and they will survive.

<u>Animal Species</u>

    Bird: Just a chicken

    As explained above, chickens are very useful for protection from the brown recluse spider and the Lonomia caterpillar. Many people consider them a necessity.

    Butterfly: Orange-barred giant sulphur   (Phoebis philea)

    In the North of Brazil, this butterfly can be seen year round, but in the South, it arrives in November and stays until the Autumn. It can be found in the forest, suburbs, and city gardens.

Spider: Brown recluse spider   (Lexosceles)

This animal has a very unpleasant bite. It hides in dark corners, beds, shoes, clothing, cupboards, etc. It bites only when disturbed, and injects an enzyme that dissolves flesh, leaving a wound that does not heal. It is found in North America as well. Curitiba, the capitol of Paranã, is the world centre for producing the antidote to the spider's bite. Each night, the bedclothes must be turned back and the bed inspected for spiders. Homes that have chickens in the gardens do not have   spiders.

Caterpillar:

Unidentified. Seen in the forest along the Estrada da Graciosa near Morretes.

Plant Species

Border: Bougainvillea   (Bougainvillea spectabilis)

Bougainvillea are native to Southern South America, and reach an enormous size, seeming to be a tree, when in truth they are vines. In *The Big Field,* Granny speaks of the purple flowers. The purple is in fact the leaves, and the flowers are tiny and white, but no one bothers to differentiate between them. They are in purple leaf from late Spring to late Autumn.

Tree: Gold medallion tree   (Cassia leptophylla)

The bright yellow flowers of this tree form great balls, the medallions of the name, throughout November. The seed to this tree appears in the story in the month of April.

Flower: Air Plant   (Tillandsia stricta)

There is a very good informational page about this lovely and little plant, with pictures, on www.rhs.org.uk. The colour of the flower is exactly that of pink bubblegum.

<u>Activities</u>

Make plant supports – With popsicle sticks, make latticework platforms. Add string to be able to hang them. Plant what is native to your region that will grow on them – lichen, mistletoe, mosses - and hang them outdoors.

Help other species too – Build a birdhouse for a local species that needs help.

Pink and Yellow flowers – Late Spring is a time inundated with pink and yellow flowers, yellow butterflies, pinkish caterpillars. Buy a few pink and yellow flowers for the classroom. Have the children make pink and yellow flowers from coloured paper. Write a poem together as a class about pink and yellow.

DECEMBER

<u>Subjects</u>

Geography – Seasons – Summer – The Summer Solstice comes just before Christmas and the New Year. Schools are closed and the children are on holiday. Days are long and very warm. It is a Brazilian custom that one must be by water when the New Year arrives. Many go to the beach, but if that is not possible, a river, lake, waterfall, or stream will do.

History and Geography – Other cultures - The custom of a candle put on a small boat and set on the water is practiced nation-wide. Candles are put in sand at the beach and flowers are thrown into the sea. All are old customs to bring good luck, health, or wealth during the next year. In *The Big Field,* Granny has added seeds, the biggest hope of all, to her New Year boats.

<u>Animal Species</u>

Bird: Red-breasted toucan   (Ramphastos dicolorus)

Toucans can be seen, rarely, in the Atlantic Rainforest, but only   deep in the forest. They stay well away from humans. But they can be heard, at dusk, their call like a squawk or yell, at times. www.xeno-canto.org has a number of recordings of their call. As toucans go, this is a small one.

Hummingbird: Black Jacobin   (Florisuga fusca)

This is one of the most easily seen of hummingbirds. In Portuguese, hummingbirds are called "flower kissers" (beija-flores), and are much loved in Brazil. Most people who live near the forest have feeders to encourage the hummingbirds to visit. They are very important to the pollination of some flowering trees, while they can also cheat and drink the nectar of others without pollinating.

| *Butterfly:* | Grecian shoemaker | (Catonephele numilia) |

| *Caterpillar:* | Killer caterpillar | (Lonomia obliqua) |

This is the caterpillar of a moth, not a butterfly. The caterpillars tend to gather around a tree, blending in with the bark. They have long hairs which, if touched, leave a poison that stops the blood coagulating. In truth, the bite of a rattlesnake is more dangerous but, if a person touches many of the caterpillars at once, as often happens if one leans against a tree where they are gathered, it can be fatal. Every child in Paranã knows to LOOK where they go.

Plant Species

| *Border:* | Morning Glory | (Convolvulus indivisus) |

Another Morning Glory!

| *Flower with toucans:* | Heliconia | (Heliconia rostrata) |

This flower hangs upside down, making it easy for hummingbirds to get its nectar.

| *Fruit:* | Brazilian cherry | (Eugenia uniflora) |

This is a very tasty fruit that has a short season. It is associated with Summer at the beach, Christmas, the New Year, and other end of year festivals. Many people spread the spicey-smelling leaves of the plant on the floors of their home to keep away flies, much as people in the Northern Hemisphere use lavender to repel insects and give a good smell to cupboards.

<u>Activities</u>

Make a sachet – Using flowers or leaves and small cloth bags, have the children fill the bags and tie them shut with ribbon.

Learn to LOOK! – Take the children on an observation walk in a garden or park, or the play area of the school, and have them look closely under plants, at the earth, in trees, and tell what they see.

Make New Year boats – These can be made of paper, and flowers instead of candles can be put on them.

THE STORY'S LAST PAGE

<u>Subjects</u>

Science – ecology – reforestation – Throughout *The Big Field,* the subtext of the child's life of discovery of nature has been the Granny's quiet determination to replant native species on her big field. Where the Southern Cross Farm was in a somewhat sterile space on the first page, here, on the last page, it is surrounded by the nature of the Atlantic Rainforest brought back to the Big Field.

History – Ourselves and our families – The story ends as the child prepares to leave Granny, go live with "Mama and Papa" and go to school in the city. Many families are dependant upon the help of a grandparent in childcare while both parents work.

<u>Animal Species</u>

Bird: Violaceous euphonia   (Euphonia violacea)

www.arthurgrosset.com has good pictures of this bird and www.xeno-canto.org has recordings of its call.

Hummingbird: Swallow-tailed hummingbird

(Eupetomena macroura)

This is one of the largest of hummingbirds and the most willing to come to bird feeders, even in apartment houses.

Again, www.arthurgrosset.com has photographs.

Butterfly: Mother-of-Pearl Morpho   (Morpho laertes)

Small butterflies: Blue silk butterfly   (Morpho anaxibia)

Caterpillar:

Unidentified tiny caterpillar, seen in Curitiba.

<u>Plant Species</u>

Border: Brazilian raspberry   (Rubus brasiliensis)

Large leaves: Pumpwood   (Cecropia pachystachya)

These trees shoot up quickly where the ground has been disturbed and at the edge of the forest. Many species of birds   like their fruit.

Red and Yellow flowers: Psychotria   (Psychotria nuda)

Large red flower: Bromeliad   (Nidularum innocentii)

<u>Activities</u>

Plant a tree: If you did not plant anything yet, now is the time. Plant a tree that is native to where you are, with all of the children helping to dig. Stake it securely, protect it, nurture it, and when the school year is over, remind the children to come back when they are grown to see it grown too.

SPECIES IN *THE BIG FIELD*

<u>Latin and English names</u>   Month

Latin and English names	Month
Actinote sp. / Lacewing	April
Anartia jatrophe / White peacock	Beginning
Araucaria angustifolia / Paranã pine	June
Atta sexsdens / Leaf cutter ants	February
Bougainvillea spectabilis / Bougainvillea	November
Bromelia / Bromeliads	July
Brotogeris tirica / Plain parakeet	May
Brunfelsia pauciflora / Yesterday-Today-and-Tomorrow	April
Calpodes ethlius / Brazilian skipper	July
Cassia leptophyla / Golden medallion tree	April,November
Catonephele numilia / Grecian shoemaker	December
Cecropia pachystachya / Pumpwood	End
Centella asiatica / Spadeleaf	April
Cepheuptychia cephus / Blue night butterfly	February
Cestrum corymbosum /Cestrum	January
Chorisia speciosa / Kapok tree	February, May
Commelina erecta / Dayflower	September
Convolvulus indivisus / Bindweed	December
Cyanocorax caeruleus / Azure jay	June
Dacnis / Blue dacnis	January
Diplopoda / Millipede	August
Dryas julia / Flame	September
Drymaeus sp. / Snail	September
Emesis mandana / Mandana metalmark	January
Emilia sonchifolia / Red tasselflower	March
Enterolobium contortisiliquum / Ear or umbrella tree	February
Erythrina falcata / Tiger's claw tree	October
Eugenia uniflora / Brazilian cherry	December

Eupetomena macroura / Swallow-tailed Hummingbird End

Euphonia violacea / Violaceous euphonia End

Ficus pumila / Creeping fig October

Fidicina mannifera / Cicada March

Furnarius rufus / Rufus Hornero or ovenbird July

Heliconia rostrata / Heliconia December

Heliconius ethilla narcaea / Helicon May

Hemiceras / Moth May

Inga sessilis / St. John's Bread Tree Macrh

Ipomea cairica / Coastal morning glory Beginning

Ipomea carnea, subs. Fistulosa / Bindweed July

Ipomea nil / Bindweed February

Ipomea purpurea / Morning glory July

Isoptera / Winged termite October

Lexosceles / Brown recluse spider November

Lonomia obliqua / Killer caterpillar December

Loranthacea / Viscum June

Melanotrochilus fuscus / Black Jacobin December

Microcentrum / Angular wing katydid June

Morpho anaxibia / Blue silk butterfly End

Morpho helenor violaceus/Common Morpho March

Morpho laertes / Mother-of-pearl morpho End

Myscelia orsis / Orsis bluewing June

Nidularium innocentii / Bromeliad End

Notiochelidon cyanoleuca / Blue-and-white swallow October

Oryctes nasicornis / Rhinoceros beetle April

Papilio sp. / Swallowtail August

Papilio anchisiades / Mourning rose January

Phasmatodea / Walking stick August

Phoebis philea / Orange-barred giant sulphur November

Pitangus sulphuratus / Great kiskadee Beginning

Procnias nudicollis / Bare-throated bell-bird October

Psychotria nuda / Psychotria	End
Ramphastos dicolorus / red breasted toucan	December
Rubus brasiliensis / Brazilian raspberry	End
Tabebuia chrysotricha / Yellow Ipê	September
Tangara seledon / Green-headed tanager	March
Tibouchina granulosa rosea / Lenten Tree	March
Tillandsia stricta / Air plant	November
Trogon surrucua / Trogon	April
Turdus rufiventris / Rufus-bellied thrush	September
Tyrannus melancholicus / Tropical kingbird	February
Tyrannus savanna / Fork-tailed flycatcher	
Vanellus chilensis / Southern lapwing	August
Wissadula subpeltata / Wissadula	August

NATURE LESSON PLANS

Comparing and Observing Nature in the
Southern and Northern Hemispheres

Whether in the city or the country, in the northern hemisphere or the southern hemisphere, there is always something to see in nature. Teaching children what to look for helps them to learn to observe. Teaching them to observe helps them to know and understand nature as a part of their world.

Following are some of the changes in nature to look for in the northern hemisphere and in the Atlantic Rainforest of southern Brazil in the southern hemisphere. For each month, there is a list of what is happening at that time in each place.

Print and use the **Nature Observation Chart** given at the end of this lesson. Children can colour it and fill in each square with a drawing or written details of what they have observed. To learn more about the hemisphere where they are not living, they can fill another with drawings of the animals and plants that they have learned are there.

January

In the northern hemisphere, it is deepest winter just now. This year has an unusual amount of snow and cold there, as all across Europe. In spite of the cold, here is what could be seen and heard outdoors:

- The White Wagtail should appear
- The Green Woodpecker will "laugh"
- Robins and Wrens are more easily seen
- The Winter Moth might still be seen in the evening
- The Dung Beetle appears
- Honeysuckle begins to leaf
- Butcher's Broom may flower
- Slugs appear

In the south of Brazil, in the southern hemisphere, it is summer, hot and humid, especially in the Atlantic Rainforest. Plants are in flowers, birds and insects are everywhere. Here are just a few of what to look for:

- The Blue Dacnis can be seen, especially at feeders
- The Mourning Rose butterfly appears
- The Orange-barred Sulphur butterfly is still about
- The Mandana Metalmark butterfly appears
- Yellow Cestrum is in flower
- Fuchsias are blooming
- Toucans can still be heard at dusk

February

Here is what those in the northern hemisphere can expect to see in February's nature:

- Moles prepare their nests
- Blackbirds are in full song
- Frogs begin to croak and spawn
- Coltsfoot flowers
- Daffodils flower late in the month

In the Atlantic Rainforest of southern Brazil and the northern part of Argentina, it is hot summertime still. In nature:

- The kapok tree is in bloom with its magnificent pink and yellow flowers shaped like stars
- Many, many trees are producing seeds
- Blue night butterflies can be seen
- The tropical kingbird is calling
- Leaf cutter ants are at their busiest, or at least seem that way

March

One of the equinoxes occurs this month, moving the seasons to autumn in the Atlantic Rainforest region of southern Brazil and to a longed-for spring in the north. As nature adjusts to a time of greater light and warmth, here is what you can expect to see in the northern hemisphere during the month of March:

- Hyacinth are in bloom
- Badgers, rabbits, field voles and lambs are born
- The Magpie and robin build their nests
- The Blackbird sits on eggs
- The Dog Violet is in flower
- Slugs pair!

In the Atlantic Rainforest region of southern Brazil, March is a time of great, late-autumn heat, when everyone feels almost unable to move because it is so hot and humid. Here is what to look for in that rainforest in March:

- Cicadas are screaming loudly everywhere and all day long
- The ingã tree is flowering
- The green-headed tanager, can be tamed with fresh bananas
- The magnificent blue morpho butterfly can be seen
- The Lenten Tree, which is native to the Atlantic Rainforest, flowers
- The tiny red tasselflower appears

April

April is a magnificent month for nature observation in most parts of the world. What you may see in the north during the month of April:

- Foxes, moles and otters are born
- The Great Bat begins to fly
- The Blue Tit builds its nest -look for it!
- The Tree Pipit should arrive in the middle of the month
- Herb Robert flowers
- The newt appears in ponds

What you may see in the southern Atlantic Rainforest in the month of April:

- Yesterday-Today-Tomorrow shows its amazing flowers
- Trogons will call
- The lacewing butterfly appears
- The golden medallion tree drops its enormous seed pods
- Oranges are ripe

May

What you may see in the north in the month of May is a flood of activity too great to list here, but some of it may be that:

- Moles are active

- Red deer and roe deer are born

- Sheep will be shorn

- Many birds build their nests: blackcaps, bullfinches, cirl buntings, corn buntings, garden warblers, the hobby falcon, jackdaws, house martins, sandpipers, swifts: This is the month to look out for nests!

- Nightjars arrive

- Plenty of insects arrive for the tasty pleasure of all those building birds: apple suckers, bee flies, moths, butterflies, dragonflies, the delightful hummingbird hawk moth

- Among the many flowers, you will see: barberry, black bryony, black medick, bugle, cleavers, holly, honeysuckle, lilac, scarlet pimpernel, sweet chestnut, yellow iris

What you may see in the southern Atlantic Rainforest of Brazil, where it is autumn and getting cold and wet and foggy, includes:

- Green parakeets in flocks

- Kapok seeds tumbling to the ground and bursting open (the silk within contains the seeds that the green parakeets love)

- Giant brown moths in swarms

- Falling leaves everywhere

- Many varieties of the helicon butterfly

June

June is the month of one of the summer/winter solstices. In the ancient Cornish language of southwestern England, it was known simply as "the summer month". In June in the northern hemisphere one can see that:

- Squirrels are born -look for their nests high in trees
- The feathers of Mallard Drakes change to resemble those of the females look for them in the ponds and lakes
- Carps spawn
- Dozens of different moths appear: Gothic moth, Goat moth, Lappet moth, Brown moth, Heart and Dart moth, Riband Wave moth, Scarlet Tiger moth
- Just about everything flowers: Lady's Fingers, Lady's Mantle, Elder, Cow Parsnip, Dogwood, Lavender, Stinking Mayweed!
- Swifts lay their eggs

In the Atlantic Rainforest of southern Brazil, June is winter, and the temperature can drop to zero degrees Celsius. The weather is wet and foggy, the rainforest dripping and sunless on many days. Now is the time the hummingbirds will come to the feeders, for there are fewer nectar-bearing flowers blooming. Yet there is much to observe in nature:

- The beautiful Orsis Bluewing butterfly is seen
- Paraná pines are dropping their huge seedballs, and monkeys are eating the seeds
- The Azure Jay also eats the seeds, and buries some for later in the season. The ones he forgets to dig up grow into trees.
- Lacewing katydids are about

July

In July, in the northern hemisphere, one can expect to see in nature:

- Harvest mice building their nests
- Weasels having their second litter
- The Cuckoo, if it still can be heard in your region, now ceases to call
- The Drinker Moth appears
- Hover flies are numerous and should remain so to the end of September
- Canterbury Bells blossom
- Golden Rod flowers
- Marjoram flowers
- Yellow Toadflax flowers
- The Grass Snake lays its eggs

In the Atlantic Rainforest of Southern Brazil, the fog can be so thick that a child will not let go of your hand for fear of being instantly lost. When the sun does come out, one can see:

- The Brazilian Skipper
- The Oven bird building its odd nest
- The Blue Ipomea purpurea flowering along the roadsides
- Bromeliads so heavy with moisture that they fall from trees with a heavy, clumping sound

August

August is well past mid-summer in the northern hemisphere and some migrants all ready are beginning to depart. In the Atlantic Rainforest no one likes August for it is always cold and dreary, but so windy that many children fly kites.

In August, in the north, children can observe in nature:

- That the Nightingales, Tree Pipits, Turtle Doves and Swifts leave
- Many insects have their second broods: Asparagus Beetles, Blood Vein Moths, Holly Blue Moths, Pine Saw-flies and Diamond-back Moths
- There are still many wildflowers, but they indicate the season to come: Autumnal Hawkbit, Autumnal Lady's-tresses, Field Gentian, Pennyroyal, Peppermint and Wormwood
- Lizards catching the warmth
- Slow-worms are born

In the cold, wet fog of the Atlantic Rainforest winter:

- Blue Swallowtail butterflies arrive
- The screeches of the Southern Lapwing echo as it protects its nest
- Millipedes are seen
- Stick insects are seen
- Hummingbirds come daily to feeders, for they suffer greatly from the cold

September

September is a month of an equinox and of noticeable migrations. There is much to observe this month. In Britain, now is when one can see that:

- Many mammals are preparing to hibernate: the Dormouse, Hedgehogs, Squirrels and the Water Vole,
- Many birds are leaving: the Blackcap, the Garden Warbler, Sand Martins, Swallows and more, and a few birds will arrive, such as Siskins,
- It is also a time to listen, for the Robin will begin to sing again, the Tawny Owl will hoot, and the Stone Curlew will clamour
- Rose hips and holly berries ripen,

In the Atlantic Rainforest, it is spring. The fog finally burns away and:

- The beautiful yellow **ipê tree** blooms and is known in folklore as the sign in nature that means the cold weather is over for another year
- The Rufus-bellied Thrush returns from its winter in the Amazon region to the north and starts to sing,
- The fork-tailed fly-catcher arrives to catch mosquitoes throughout the summer,
- The beautiful bright orange butterfly called the Flame appears.

October

In the northern hemisphere, October is early to mid-autumn. There is much to see as animals and plants prepare to protect themselves during the harsher cold weather to come --by storing food, preparing to hibernate or become dormant, or moving on to warmer climes. There:

- The Common Shrew prepares its winter nest
- Field Voles prepare to hibernate
- Goldfinches visit thistleheads for seeds
- The Hooded Crow arrives
- Frogs hibernate, as do Grass Snakes and Toads
- Walnuts ripen

In the Atlantic Rainforest, October means rain, and rain and rain. It is springtime and the rain is almost warm. As nature awakens from its very short winter, colour abounds.

- The native Tiger Claw tree blooms
- The swallows return from the north
- Termites rise on wing from mounds as high as a child of seven is tall
- The magnificent, metallic call of the Bare-Throated Bell-bird can be heard ringing in the forest
- Butterflies and beetles appear in great number

November

In the north, it is deep enough into autumn that no trace of summer really remains. In the south, springtime is surging toward summer with a life force that is heady. In the north, here is what can be observed in the month of November:

- Bucks are grunting
- Fieldfares and Redwings are feeding, sometimes together, on hips and haws (rose hips and hawthorn berries)
- Greenfinches begin to flock
- Ash leaves fall
- Hazel catkins become conspicuous

In the Atlantic Rainforest of South America, one can now see:

- The magnificent orange-barred giant sulphur butterfly
- The highly poisonous Brown spider
- Golden medallion trees are in bloom
- Bougainvillea, called Primavera, blooms pink or purple
- The bright pink Tillandsia stricta

December

December marks the end of the calendar year and the beginning of a new season: summer in the south and winter in the north. With such deeply different seasons, people grow up with profoundly different associations with this time of year. For those in the southern hemisphere, December and its festivals is a time of sunny, hot days, going to the beach, the long and lazy school holiday, and outdoor cooking, while in the north it is a time of bundling up, baking pies and cookies, sitting indoors before the fire. The differences in nature are just as dramatic.

In the northern hemisphere:

- Foxes, searching for food, are seen much more often
- Where it is cold, the Stoat assumes its white coat to become an Ermine
- Yellow buntings congregate in flocks
- The Wren can be heard singing
- Holly berries are easy to see
- Winter aconite flowers

In the Atlantic Rainforest:

- Grecian Shoemaker butterflies appear
- Toucans call out in the evening
- Black Jacobin Hummingbirds appear
- The Pitanga fruit is ripe
- The lethal Lonomia caterpillar appears

Nature Observation Chart

©2020 Anne Morddel

THREE JAYS PLANTING ON THREE CONTINENTS

While it is exciting to learn about the different animals, weather and seasons of the other hemisphere, it can also be quite comforting for children to learn of the similarities. When it comes to the raucous, bounding jay, there are many.

- The Blue Jay of North America is a generic term for at least five species (*Cyanocitta*), all of which have extensive blue colouring.

- The Jay of Europe (*Garrulus glandarius*) , shown below, has just a tiny patch of blue, as if his cousins across the Atlantic had sent him a handkerchief of theirs.

- The Azure Jay (*Cyanocorax caeruleus*) of South America's Atlantic Rainforest (below) is like a regal relative with a deep blue cloak and a black hood.

All are members of the crow family and it shows in their personalities. All are so well known for their habit of hiding seeds that they have become almost symbolic for it in each region.

In late summer and early autumn when seeds from the great trees are falling, the jays on all three continents are greedy about trying to find as many seeds as possible to store. They hide them in logs, under leaves, in the earth, in anticipation of the lean times to come during the winter. Some they find later and eat; some they do not. Those they do not find often germinate and grow into trees. To people observing them, it seems as if they are intentionally planting the seeds and many stories about them doing so are told. In a time when forests are disappearing, reforestation has taken on urgency and almost a sacredness. The jays, once reviled for their greed, (among other anti-social habits) have become something of the eco-hero.

- The Blue Jay's preferred seed is one of the many types of North American oak acorn, though he is not fussed.

- The European Jay also prefers the acorn of the oak (*Quercus ilex*).

- The Azure jay's seed is that of the Paraná pine tree (*Aurucaria angustifolia*) which are about double the size of a big acorn and which are called in Portuguese pinhão (pronounced "pin-YOW"). This jay is more at risk of extinction than the others for, as the Paraná pine is extensively logged and as people and monkeys also love the seeds, this beautiful bird has nothing left to eat.

Some Ways To Share The Three Jays With Children

Mark a Map - Print out the pictures of the jays from this post and attach them to their correct locations on a map of the world.

Game - Play a version of "Button, button, whose got the button?" – In advance, either use real acorns and a pinhão or make seeds from card. Make as many of each seed as there are children. Make three paper baskets and attach to each a picture of one of the jays. To play, have the children sit in a circle, facing inward, with their hands behind their backs. Place the three baskets in the centre. Select one child to begin.

Give that child one seed so that the others cannot see what it is. That child goes around the outside of the circle, while everyone chants "Seed, seed, who's got the seed?" During the chant, the child must place the seed into the hands of another, then keep walking until the chant stops and sit down in the circle. The child with the seed must stand and place the pinhão or acorn in the basket of the bird that would eat it. The teacher gives this child a new seed, again so that the others cannot see it, and the game is played again, until each child has had at least one chance.

Help the jays plant trees!

If you provide the jays with more seeds, their instinct will lead them to take them and store them, thus increasing their food store for the winter, and also increasing the chance that more seeds will germinate and grow into trees.

Jays like open platforms as feeders, not anything with a cover or little roof. You can hang a tray from a branch, or nail one to the top of a post. Ours is nailed to the top of an arbour. It does need to be sturdy, for jays are not tiny birds. With the children, gather acorns and pinhões to put on the tray. It is important that the seeds be green, or as much so as possible, for they will have a better chance of germinating.

Make Jay Beanbags or Colour Some Jays and Make a Mobile

Use the pictures either as templates to cut fabric, have the children sew it and fill with beans to make bean bags OR to colour the jays and cut out to make a mobile.

A SOUTH-NORTH SEASONS TABLE

A nature table is a display of natural things children have found outdoors and brought into the classroom or home. The item is identified and the child writes a label for it and puts it on the table with the other contributions. Feathers, stones, seeds, bones, shells, flowers, anything natural qualifies, though there are rules against uprooting protected plants, stealing eggs from nests, etc. If they cannot go outdoors, they can make and draw what they would find. The table or shelf is ideally at a low enough level such that the children can view the items easily. The benefits to the children are important:

- They relate their learning to real nature and not merely photographs in a book

- They know that what they find will be admired and included in the class's display

- They become both more observant and knowledgeable when they are outdoors

In Ann Druitt's book, *All Year Round : a Calendar of Celebration*, the seasons table is enlivened with small soft figures placed among the seeds and stones, creating a complete scene.

Why not try a variation on the theme that will require a bit of ingenuity on everyone's part? One that shows items from nature's display during the current seasons in both the southern and northern hemispheres. The table could begin with summer in the south and late winter in the north. Here's how:

Location - select a table or shelf low enough for the children to see easily. It should not be in a remote corner, far from the class, but central, so that it can be easily seen and discussed.

Preparation - Cover the table with two simple cloths, half the table a colour associated with summer, such as bright green or yellow, the other half with a colour associated with winter, such as grey or white for snow. You may wish to put a divider of some sort between the two different cloths, something to represent the ocean, perhaps. This could be a strip of blue paper cut out and

decorated with fish, boats, shells, etc. or something more solid such as a block of wood painted blue with shells glued to it. Alternatively, you might use a bit of driftwood to signify mountains as a divider. If the location allows, a backcloth hanging above the table to represent the sky increases the interest. This could be half blue and half white or grey again. Children can stick up clouds, rain clouds, snow, etc. as the weather changes.

Using the South-North Seasons Table - Take the children or encourage them to go into the garden, to the park, etc. and teach them to observe. If you are in the southern hemisphere, now is a time of flowers, seeds, leaves, empty birds' nests, insect casings. If in the northern hemisphere, it is a time of bare branches, small buds, early bulbs, bark, perhaps sap beginning to run, mosses. Allow for the ugly: the dead bug, the bleached skull, as for some children this is much more interesting than the "pretty". Bring back what you can, find the correct name for it. You can even begin to teach children the basics of scientific naming and how important it is.

Do not just dump the items on the table and forget them. Relate them to lessons, find poems about them, encourage the children to make pictures of them - an experiment in still life drawing – and learn more about what they have found. Keep going out and finding more and adding to the table, changing the display as the season progresses.

For the hemisphere that is not yours, try to visit a botanical garden near by, if you have one. If you are in the north, any florist will have a tropical plant or two. If you cannot buy the plant, you may be able to ask for some of the leaves it has dropped. Have the children draw butterflies and make paper birds of the other hemisphere to put on the table. If you have a zoo close by, take the children or encourage them to go and to see the animals and birds there from the opposite hemisphere.

Here are some good websites to help you find animals and plants from the two hemispheres:

For the northern hemisphere - http://www.birdsofbritain.co.ukThis will even give the calls of some birds.

For the southern hemisphere - http://www.arthurgrosset.comOne of the very best sites for South American birds.

For both hemispheres - http://www.nhm.ac.ukThis is the Natural History Museum's wonderful site.

MASKED BIRDS

Learning about animal characteristics can help children to learn to observe. As children learn outdoor observation activities, they can begin to make comparisons. Here is one example.

Many animals and birds have colouring that looks to us like eye masks. The Blue Dacnis (*Dacnis cayana*) in the Atlantic Rainforest of South America, the Masked Laughingthrush (*Garrulax perspicillatus*) in Asia, and some of the nuthatches (*Sitta europaea* and *Sitta canadensis*) in Europe and North America all are examples of birds with a black band across their eyes:

- The Blue Dacnis

- The Masked Laughingthrush

- The Nuthatch

Biologists do not really know why that type of colouring evolved. The strongest theory is that it makes the eyes (and thus the bird) seem larger and that predators will be scared off. That makes sense for masks that look like huge circles around the eyes, but we are not so sure about the type of mask that looks like a bandit's. Such a marking does not make the eyes seem bigger; it makes them seem to disappear. Perhaps that scares predators too.

In a class discussion, we asked children (aged 6-7) why they thought birds would have such a mask across their faces. Here are some of the responses:

• Maybe it is some kind of a crook
• So the bugs could not see it eat them
• It looks cool

Make bird masks

All you need is a roll of black crepe paper. Cut a strip for each child. Let them cut eye holes, and tie the strip around their heads. Ask them to choose which of the four masked birds above they want to be, and to draw a picture of it.

To help them decide, if you have classroom computers and the internet, go to the Internet Bird Collection https://www.hbw.com/ibc

and look at some videos of them. Remember to type the Latin name into

the search box to get straight to the correct bird.

Discussion

Ask the children why they think these birds have such a masking. Get them discussing and exchanging ideas.

Extend the observation

The next time you go outdoors or look out the window, ask the children to look for other similarities in colouring in nature.

WHAT IS A WEED? WHAT IS A FLOWER?

In our gardens and yards, we teach our children that weeds are bad and flowers are good. By doing so we do them and nature a terrible disservice. There is a specific definition for flower : "that part of a plant comprising a group of reproductive organs and its envelopes". There is no such scientific clarity for a weed: "a herbaceous plant not valued for use or beauty". A flower may or may not be pretty but it has a clear function for the plant. To call something a weed is basically to say that one does not like that plant.

Most people tend to say that what grows naturally on their patch of ground are "weeds" and what they have planted themselves are "flowers". (How that encapsulates the essence of humanity's battle against nature!) We nurture what they want and kill or pull up what they do not want. Too often, what we tend to plant is something from another part of the world, something we have admired and want to have, even if our climate and soil are nothing like that plant's natural environment. Too often, the weeds we poison and pull up are food for the insects, birds, and creatures around us. Sometimes they can eat what we plant, but not often, and people do not like it when they do. Sometimes, they can move on to where native plants still exist, but we then have less of nature around us and fewer animals can survive on the reduced food source. Sometimes they are poisoned by what we import and they eat.

In the northern hemisphere, if gardeners finally succeed in getting rid of every last stinging nettle (*Urtica dioica*), they will also get rid of the beautiful peacock butterfly (*Inochis io*), whose caterpillars eat nettles.

In South America, if every clump of boring green with tiny, insignificant flowers is removed then the creature that needs it in order to survive will also be removed. Permanently.

Our habit of despising the home-grown and desiring the exotic in our gardens does ill to the environment in other ways as well. Native plants need little care, soil changes, or extra water, while exotic or foreign plants usually need extra water and fertilizers. This is when we live in a time of increasing water shortage and soil pollution and need to conserve water and keep the soil healthy.

We often read about the numerous plants in the rainforest that are being destroyed before they can have been fully identified and their properties discovered. Thus, despising what is local and native in favour of what is exotic, foreign, and maybe profitable, has meant that plants of potential medical value have been lost. The little blue flower (*Stachytarpheta elatior*) shown above is a perfect example. It is native to Brazil. Farmers consider it a serious nuisance because it grows easily and very densely and they kill it whenever they can. It is a food source for the Mourning Rose butterfly (*Papilio anchisiades*) shown above. It is also considered to be of medicinal value; its leaves are used to make a tea to treat hepatitis.

We teach children to cherish or at least appreciate nature while at the same time we destroy it. What is more, by destroying what is native, that which is their own environment, we devalue their world to them and teach them that only the exotic and cultivated is valuable. How can we then ask them to preserve nature? How to clarify this and give them a clearer message and understanding?

Start a Native/Non-Native or South/North Garden

Gardening and discovering how plants grow is all ready a part of the Early Years curriculum, but the activity can be greatly enhanced by using it to teach about the importance of native species.

Preparation - You will be creating a garden that will have two distinct halves. Plan to plant some seeds of local native plants. Then, look for seeds or seedlings of exotic plants from the hemisphere opposite to yours. To find seeds and seedlings, try mail-order seed companies as well as garden shops and markets. CAUTION - be sure to select only those plants of which no part is poisonous or an allergen.

Location - Are you fortunate enough to have space outdoors for a real garden? Wonderful! One way to make it much easier and more enjoyable for small children is to garden is to do so on raised beds of hay. With hay, it is possible to put earth on top and plant into that. The hay serves as a mulch to protect the seedlings from other plants swamping them. As it decomposes, it enriches the soil organically. No digging or tilling is required and raised beds are just the right height for little gardeners. Best of all, when the hay is delivered, it is great fun to jump on it and stamp it into place. WARNING - Some children may be allergic to hay and may have to miss out on the jumping part. If you do not have a plot for your class, two window boxes will do. Even two pots will do. Label one native and the other non-native. For the natives to thrive, they should be as close to the real environment as possible, so do not put them in a dark corner or on top of the heater or air conditioner!

Gardening - Plant your seeds. Care for them. Learn about your plants. Get someone from one of the local garden clubs who specializes in native species of plants to come and give a talk to the class. Observe your plants. What insects or birds or other animals use them for food or housing? How much care do the native plants need? How much care do the non-natives need? How much water do they need? Which ones thrive? Do the local insects like any of the non-natives? They may well do. (Remember, one of Europe's most popular shrubs, the "butterfly bush", or buddleia, is native to Asia.)

Discuss - If a plant becomes covered with mites or a fungus, find out more about it. The fungus lives off of the plant and leads to its death and decomposition. Is that its function in nature? Is there a parasite of the fungus? Or of the mites? Try to help the children see that nature is interconnectedness. Like that old song about the bones ("the knee bone's connected to the thigh bone, the thigh bone's connected to the hip bone," and so on) the earth, the water, the sun, the plant, the things that feed off the plant and are in turn food for others, all are interconnected.

By learning that interconnectedness, they will begin to learn to appreciate each part of nature in its own place. With that appreciation, they will be better equipped to live within and preserve nature.

LOW DOWN LOOKING

If lying on one's back and gazing at clouds is good for the artistic imagination in us all, lying on one's tummy and gazing at tiny life forms is good for our inner scientific observer. Further to developing children's observation skills, plan a session of "low down looking".

To prepare the children for the concept of observation, ask the children if they have ever seen a spider. One assumes they will all shout "Yes!" Now, ask them if they have ever watched a spider build its entire web. I could be wrong here, but I would guess not. The point is that they need to begin to be aware of the difference between *seeing* and *observing*.

Low Down Looking Activity

All you will need are:

- a guide to local insects and wildflowers from the library
- paper and pencil for each child

Go outdoors together and have everyone lie on their tummies, (or gaze out a window, if you cannot go out, or watch a nature film online of closeup images) with paper and pencils ready for sketching what they see. (Be careful not to have the children lay on unpleasant plants such as nettles or poison oak!) Remind the children that this is a time of observation, so they are not to trap or disturb what they see. Encourage each child to draw an insect or plant as accurately as possible, trying to get the right number of eyes and legs.

As each drawing is finished, help the children to find their plant or insect in the guide. Some children will be better at using the guides; some will be better at drawing. They can help one another in striving for accuracy.

Have you no green place on which to lie? Is your play area concrete? Look around. There are probably plants that have pushed their way through some cracks. Have the children observe there and be amazed at life's perseverance.

Cannot find your bug? Go to the Bug Forum on the website of the Natural History Museum and ask an expert. (https://www.nhm.ac.uk/discover.html?q=gallery)

Repeat this activity in other locations, on class visits to city farms, orchards, zoos, etc.

At the end of the season, with the children, tally how many times each species was observed and make a display of the results : your local bug population.

LEARNING TO OBSERVE

When we take children outdoors to gather things and then back inside to paint them; when we go outdoors to find things and bring them inside to build something with them, we are not teaching observation - the first and most essential skill of science and poetry. We are teaching technology or art. The former is applied science; the latter is the imitation of nature. None of these, neither science nor poetry, nor technology nor art will be a successful endeavor without a developed capacity for observation.

In understanding the human world and its machines and machinations, we teach children to ask and find the answers to :

- Who?
- What?
- Where?
- When?
- Why?
- How?

To understand nature and the physical world around us, we use our five senses:

- Sight
- Hearing
- Touch
- Smell
- Taste

In spite of all of our capacity to gather, store, and exchange information, it is an augmentation of knowledge, and no replacement for the knowledge we acquire first hand through our senses. If anything is disastrous about our children's modern existence of television, cinema, electronic games, the internet and all the rest of it, it is the failure to develop the use of their senses. Spatial concepts and the ability to calculate faster may be more developed, but the ability to recognize a variety of sounds, colours, flavours, odours, and textures -- the ability to participate in life -- is being lost.

Not only must we teach children to observe; we must teach them to observe honestly. Before a fact can be interpreted, it has to be observed with clarity. On seeing a tree in bloom with pink flowers, we must first see it for what it is, tall or short, healthy or sick, light pink or dark, with leaves or without, etc. before we can write a poem about it or paint it, or calculate its value as timber. If we do not observe, and clearly and honestly, our knowledge will be hollow and our decisions will be mistakes.

Our children have a right and a responsibility to know the world first hand. As more and more of them live lives indoors, they will not have days of free play outdoors in tall grasses or on a beach or in a wood. Increasing numbers of children will never have long hours outdoors of gazing, watching, seeing, idly staring, doing nothing at all but just looking at things such as clouds, bugs, birds, frogs, streams. They will not have the opportunity to learn naturally how to observe. We will have to teach them.

Learning To Observe Nature

This exercise will use four senses only. There will be no tasting!

You will need:
• a sheet of clear plastic, about 30cm x 40cm, such as are often found

in inexpensive picture frames
• an empty picture frame or a substitute cut from sturdy card

Taking these, go outdoors with the children. Find a quiet place to sit near some greenery. Lead the children as a group in the close observation of just one thing, such as a tree, shrub, bird, log, flower. Let them look at, touch, smell, listen to it. Ask questions based on the senses, e.g.:

What do we see?
• What colour is it?
• Is it big or small?
• Is it fat or thin?

• What shape is it?

• How many branches or leaves or petals has it?

What do we smell?

• Is it a sweet smell?

• A rancid smell?

• Is the smell strong or faint?

• Does it make your eyes water?

What do we hear?

• A birdsong?

• Movement?

• Is it loud or soft?

• A tinkling? A rustling? A scratching?

What can we feel?

• Is it rough or smooth?

• Soft or hard?

• Squishy? Gritty?

• Hot or cold?

• Wet or Dry?

As you go through this exercise, you will at the same time be greatly enlarging the children's vocabulary. Do this two or three times as a group, observing different things. Then, let each child try giving a full observation on his or her own. Encourage as much description and detail of true perceptions as possible. Encourage the use of the correct words for each perception. Lead the children away from comparison to other things they know. (e.g. "It smells like my dog" or "It looks like my toy.") Comparison and analogy come later. First, one must be able to observe.

To take the exercise further, hold up the plastic in front of something that has all ready been observed. This will have the effect of flattening the view of it as if it were a photograph. Ask the children how this separation from the object changes how they see, hear, smell, and feel it. Then, hold up the empty frame instead of the plastic. This has the effect of narrowing the focus and for some people helps them to observe better. Ask them again how the frame changes how they perceive the object.

Ideally, this should be done at least once a week. As the year progresses, the children's powers of observation will greatly improve, along with their vocabulary and their ability to concentrate. Besides that, it's fun.

N.B. For an example of wonderful powers of clear and honest observation, read a few passages of Darwin's *Voyage of the Beagle*. Though it is not about teaching, it is a lesson in observation.

SEASONS AND MONTHS AROUND THE WORLD

SEASONS OUT AND NORTH	SUMMER	DRY SEASON	RAINY SEASON	AUTUMN	WINTER	DRY SEASON	RAINY SEASON	SPRING
Europe	June July August			September October November	December January February			March April May
North America	June July August			September October November	December January February			March April May
India	April May June		April May June July August	July August September	October November December		November December January February March	February March
China	May June July			July August September October	November December January February			March April
Equatorial Africa		December January	February March April			May, June July August	September October November	
Amazon Region	February, March April, May June		January to December		July	May to October (not really dry, but less rain)		
Northern Australia (Top End)	April . October		November December	May June	July	August September October	January February	March
South America	December January February			March April May	June July August			September October November
Southern Australia	December January February			March April May	June July August			September October November
Southern Africa	November December		January February March	April	May, June July August	May June July August	September October November December	September October

A CHILD'S SECURITY
IN THE FACE OF CLIMATE CHANGE

Fairly regularly now, someone writes in the press of their concern for how much children are being frightened by all the dire talk about climate change or global warming. It *is* frightening. Many adults are frightened as well, though they tend to respond with anger more than with tears and bad dreams. (Perhaps.) Leo Hickman wrote in the Guardian's "Green Living Blog" a post entitled "Are Global Warming and Deforestation Too Scary for Sesame Street?" In it, he discusses how many television shows and publications for children find the subject too frightening to address. An earlier Guardian article along these lines is Bjorn Lomborg's "Scared Silly Over Climate Change". He gives examples of frightened and confused children and insists that the press report in a less terrifying manner.

That will never happen. Terror, horror and appealing to our morbid curiosity are what sell the news. It is up to us as teachers, librarians, and parents to find the solid ground for our children in this sea of fear and confusion.

It is not my intention here to sink into the bog of defending or disputing the claims about climate change, but I do intend to look at the facts so that we can help our children. What is indisputable is that:

• there is a serious crisis of overpopulation of our species, and
• there is a serious crisis of pollution of every part of the planet

Our children will have to live with these things and try to amend the situation. We must give them the clarity, strength, courage, and example to do so.

When children are frightened, they take their security from certainties. There can be no greater certainties than the cycles of the seasons, the months, and days. These are easily explained to children as brought about by the sun, the earth's orbit around it, the earth's tilt on its axis, the moon's orbit around the earth, and the earth's spinning on its axis. Yes, science tells us that the sun will one day burn out, but computer models estimate that will happen in 4 or more billion years, rather a long time from now.

Let's begin with a definition of "forever" as being at least a million years. Thus, we can safely tell children that all of the following are forever:

- The sun will be in the sky, so we will always have light
- The earth will always orbit the sun and earth's axis will be tilted, so we will always have seasons
- The moon will circle the earth, so we will always have waves in the seas
- The earth will turn on its axis, so we will always have days and nights

As you teach geography, point out this aspect of permanence. When children ask questions about climate change, the future of the planet, pollution, etc., remind them of what is permanent. With this solidity, you can more comfortably discuss how we must address the issues of concern, remembering to keep the discussion appropriate to their level of understanding:

• The night sky will always have stars, but we may not be able to see them because of air pollution. They are still there. What could we all do to reduce air pollution so that we can see the stars again? This could lead to activities aimed at discovering causes of air and light pollution, perhaps a night class with a telescope, perhaps charts showing how turning off lights not only saves electricity but reduces light pollution.

- Here is the very useful education page of the International Dark Sky Association (https://www.darksky.org/) which has some good downloads
- For this and the following topics, the EcoSchools (http://www.eco-schools.org.uk) programme is an excellent resource

• The seasons – summer, autumn, winter, spring – will always occur and always in that order, though they may be hotter and rainier than in the past because of too much carbon in the atmosphere. How can we reduce the carbon and increase the oxygen? This particular discussion could be expanded to include tree-planting, via one of the many, many programmes now in existence.

- The Plant a Billion Trees site (http://www.plantabillion.org) teaches about trees of the Atlantic Rainforest and accepts donations.

• The moon will always be in the sky and will always circle the earth, pulling the oceans with its gravity and making waves. The waves will always be there, but they might be full of rubbish or empty of fish because of pollution or the waters warming. How can we clean up the rivers and oceans and stop polluting them? This discussion could lead to involvement in some of the many programmes for cleaning up beaches, rescuing sea birds and animals, etc.

- The UK Rivers Network (https://www.ukrivers.net/education.html) has some good resources dealing with pollution

- The Ocean Project (http://www.theoceanproject.org)

is full of information and ideas on how to save the oceans

By consistently teaching what is permanent we can approach our problems with greater confidence, and help our children to see their future not with fear but with hope.

Finding Security In Nature's Repetitions

Using the solstices as an illustration, we can move to the next of the most fundamental lessons of nature: repetition.

Repetition is observed everywhere in nature. The seasonal cycle repeats. The

processes of seeds falling, germinating, sprouting leaves, growing into plants

repeat. The moon's cyclical waxing and waning repeats. There are millions of species identified and all of them have repetition in their behaviour as animals and development as plants. It is repetition that gives us an almost inborn certainty that nothing ends forever but will begin again. For small children, this is a source of comfort and security.

Learning to observe it in nature is also the beginning of developing an enquiring mind. Encourage children to keep track of the phases of the moon all year long. Above the nature table, keep a cut-out moon that is at the same phase as is the real moon. Go outdoors (or online) and look for repetition - in a plant's repeat flowering, in the way all of the flowers on a plant are the same, in the way ants all repeat the to and- fro of food gathering along the same path. There are innumerable examples. Help the children to find something that is repeating and to draw it or write about it.

Solstices repeat twice a year. They mark the days when the sun is as far from the zenith as it can go before it begins to move slowly back again. Put differently, it is the day when summer and winter have reached their midway point in their respective hemispheres.

Where it is the winter solstice, people for centuries in both the northern and

southern hemispheres have celebrated the day as a turning point, a time when the shortening of days ceases and long hours of darkness begin to lessen. Various symbols and rituals celebrate that the time of cold, trees without leaves, no flowers, animals either hibernating or gone -- in short, the time of dying -- has stopped, and spring, with all of its life, will return. In many pre-Christian societies, from New Zealand to Norway, the winter solstice was the beginning of the new year.

Where it is the summer solstice, it is the peak of life, fruition and flowering. Again, there are celebrations, midnight fires, a heady exultation in the plenitude of nature. The same sense of it being a turning point is present, though in the summer it is usually with poignancy and the awareness that the days will begin to grow shorter and colder. Then, leaves will fall, birds will migrate, animals will hibernate, until it will seem that the whole world has died. Then, with spring, it will come to life again.

The repetitions of the solstices and equinoxes will go on forever. Knowing this, looking for it and for other repetitions, will help to give children the security from nature that they need in order to face the future and deal with the environmental problems that are ahead.

Security From Nature's Patterns

After permanence and repetition, one of nature's most important and beautiful lessons is pattern. Nature is not chaos; nature is pattern and the compulsion to pattern. Whether a spider's web, bodily construction, petal arrangement in flowers, patterning is everywhere, within and without. Our need to reason is, ultimately, our need to see and understand the pattern of something.

Teaching a child to observe the patterns in nature will help even further to develop an enquiring mind. Begin with the simplest: pairs in our construction. We have two eyes, two ears, two nostrils, two arms, two legs. With pictures of animals, including birds and insects, discuss pairs in our structure with children.

Move on to plants, where pattern continues but is different. Look at the veins in leaves, which branch off from a central trunk, sometimes opposite, sometimes alternate. Look at flowers that may have three, four, five six, or more petals. Look at the fur of the big cats, the wings of butterflies. Go outdoors and let each child tell of a pattern he or she can observe. There are thousands of workbook pages teaching pattern recognition. The origin is nature, so why not use that? It is much more attractive and fun and better rooted in reality.

Being able to observe a pattern, recognize its structure leads the mind to be able to predict what the pattern maker will do next. Correct prediction is integral to scientific discovery. Using something as simple as a vine, help your observers to look at how the leaves grow along it, while you keep the end covered. Slowly revealing more, let them predict where the next leaf will be -- opposite, alternate, in twos or singular. With something as simple as a flower, point out how the buds grow, examine the opened flowers, lead the children to predict how the flowers will look when the other buds open. Repeat exercises like this many times with many different plants and animals, until the children begin to tell you of their independent observations of pattern, and find security in being able to "figure out" about, on a basic level, the world around them.

Permanence, repetition and pattern are what we can observe in nature. They are solid facts on which children can begin to build a sense of certainty about the natural world. Teach them to see the absolute permanence of the seasons, night and day, and they will learn security. Teach them to see the repetition and pattern and they will learn to reason well. Teach them to love the beauty of nature, and they will want to preserve it